Great Artists
Raphael

Adam G. Klein

ABDO
Publishing Company

visit us at
www.abdopublishing.com

Published by ABDO Publishing Company, 4940 Viking Drive, Edina, Minnesota 55435.
Copyright © 2007 by Abdo Consulting Group, Inc. International copyrights reserved in all
countries. No part of this book may be reproduced in any form without written permission from
the publisher. The Checkerboard Library™ is a trademark and logo of ABDO Publishing
Company.

Printed in the United States.

Cover Photo: Corbis
Interior Photos: Art Resource pp. 1, 4, 5, 10, 11, 13, 15, 16, 17, 19, 20, 22, 23, 27; Bridgeman
    Art Library pp. 21, 25, 26; Corbis p. 9; Getty Images pp. 14, 29

Series Coordinator: Megan M. Gunderson
Editors: Megan M. Gunderson, Megan Murphy
Art Direction: Neil Klinepier

Library of Congress Cataloging-in-Publication Data

Klein, Adam G., 1976-
  Raphael / Adam G. Klein.
    p. cm. -- (Great artists)
  Includes index.
  ISBN-10 1-59679-734-7
  ISBN-13 978-1-59679-734-5
  1. Raphael, 1483-1520--Juvenile literature. 2. Painters--Italy--Biography--Juvenile literature. I.
Raphael, 1483-1520. II. Title III. Series: Klein, Adam G., 1976- . Great artists.
  ND623.R2K54 2006
  759.5--dc22

                                                                    2005017892

Contents

Raphael

Raphael is a famous artist from the Renaissance. During the Renaissance, the worlds of art and science made major advancements. This was a time of learning and exploration. And, there was a renewed interest in **antiquity** during this period.

Like many artists of his time, Raphael excelled in more than one art form. He is known for his Madonna portraits. But, he also painted **frescoes** and was a skilled **architect**. Raphael's experimentation with style and medium was influenced by the time period he lived in.

Raphael often did "studies," or drawings, before creating a fresco.

The Madonna del Granduca *is just one example of Raphael's many Madonna portraits. The soft lighting shows thoughtful faces and the loving relationship between mother and child.*

Raphael's accomplishments are a great example of what people can achieve. Since his death almost 500 years ago, few have matched his talent and genius. And today, he continues to inspire people toward greatness.

Timeline

1483 ~ On April 6, Raphael was born in Urbino, Italy.

1499 ~ Raphael painted a two-sided work for a church in Città di Castello.

1504 ~ Raphael painted the *Marriage of the Virgin*; Raphael traveled to Florence.

1507 ~ Raphael painted *The Entombment*.

1508 ~ Raphael moved to Rome.

1509 ~ Raphael began the Stanza della Segnatura frescoes; Pope Julius II hired Raphael as *scriptor brevium*.

1512 ~ Raphael painted *The Triumph of Galatea* for Agostino Chigi.

1512 to 1513 ~ Raphael created the *Sistine Madonna*.

1514 ~ Raphael was hired as the new architect of St. Peter's Basilica.

1517 ~ Pope Leo X put Raphael in charge of preserving Roman antiquities.

1519 ~ Raphael's Sistine Chapel tapestries were completed.

1520 ~ Raphael died on April 6 before finishing the *Transfiguration*.

Fun Facts

- Raphael was excited to have the chance to travel to Rome. When he left Florence, he left behind a public commission unfinished and unpaid!

- In addition to his involvement with painting and architecture, Raphael had plans to create a map of ancient Rome and large sculptures.

- The Sistine Chapel is named after Pope Sixtus IV. Raphael's painting the *Sistine Madonna* gets its name from the figure of Saint Sixtus II, who was also a pope.

- Raphael painted the Stanza della Segnatura frescoes at the same time Michelangelo was painting the ceiling of the Sistine Chapel. When Michelangelo took a break, Raphael asked to finish the ceiling! Even though Michelangelo would rather have been sculpting, this offer did not make him very happy. Later, Michelangelo claimed Raphael had learned everything he knew from him.

Urbino

Raphael was born Raffaello Sanzio on April 6, 1483, in Urbino, Italy. His father, Giovanni Santi, was a painter for the **court** of Urbino. Raphael's mother, Magia di Battista Ciarla, died on October 7, 1491. His father died a few years later on August 1, 1494.

Around this time, Urbino was becoming a **cultural** and political center with great vision. In the court of Urbino, Raphael was exposed to some of the best artists and thinkers from around the world. Because of his father's connections in the court, Raphael began training to be an artist.

Raphael's first-known work was a two-sided banner for a church in Città di Castello, a town near Urbino. The work is dated around 1499. It shows Raphael's early talent and most likely helped him earn other assignments.

In 1500, Raphael was only 17 years old. This is probably why he shared his first major **commission** with an artist from his

Urbino is located in central Italy.

father's workshop. Raphael and Evangelista da Pian di Meleto created an **altarpiece** together. It was for the Church of Saint Agostino in Città di Castello. Still, Raphael had much to learn.

Raphael soon gained the skills he needed to find his own work as an artist. By 1501, he had left Urbino and traveled to Perugia. There, he became associated with the well-known Italian artist Pietro Perugino. Perugino had worked in the Sistine Chapel just 20 years earlier. He was considered a master of **frescoes**.

Raphael's style took on **characteristics** of Perugino's work. One of Raphael's first major works was the *Marriage of the Virgin*, from 1504. It was

The clear, simple style of Giving of the Keys to St. Peter *was an early example of Renaissance ideals.*

influenced by Perugino's *Giving of the Keys to St. Peter*, which is in the Sistine Chapel.

Raphael had worked in Perugia for many years. While there, Perugino had taught him about the business of art. Eventually, some people could hardly tell their work apart. But slowly, Raphael's work had become superior to the work of his master.

***Raphael's figures in the* Marriage of the Virgin *are more lifelike than those in Perugino's* Giving of the Keys to St. Peter.**

Florence

In 1504, Raphael traveled to nearby Florence. He wanted to continue improving his work, and the city was an ideal place to study. In Florence, Raphael met Michelangelo di Lodovico Buonarroti Simoni and Leonardo da Vinci. The three artists are considered masters of the Renaissance.

Michelangelo and Leonardo were competitive. Leonardo was known for his expressive subjects and his knowledge of science. Michelangelo was known for the emotional style of his work. Raphael benefited from being close to both artists. He took their best ideas and used them in his own work.

In 1507, Raphael created another famous work, *The Entombment*. It showcased all the skills he had learned in Florence. And, *The Entombment* proved that he could successfully paint large works. This would be very important later in his career.

The Entombment *became so famous that it was stolen 100 years after it was created.*

Raphael worked hard to improve his art. In Florence, he mostly created portraits, **altarpieces**, and smaller religious paintings. He had both public and private **commissions**. And, his reputation as an artist grew quickly. But, he still had to make a name for himself in Rome.

Rome

During the Renaissance, Pope Julius II **commissioned** artists to work in Rome. He was fulfilling a vision to re-create Rome as the **cultural** center of the world. His master plan included building a new church, St. Peter's Basilica. Once completed, it would become one of the greatest buildings in the world.

Raphael moved to Rome in 1508. He followed many artists, poets, philosophers, and musicians, including Michelangelo and the **architect** Donato Bramante. They all wanted to work for the Catholic Church. The church was one of the greatest **patrons** of the arts.

Raphael was dazzled by Rome. Many of the ancient **artifacts** and buildings

St. Peter's Basilica took more than 100 years to complete.

Even before he traveled to Rome, Raphael was interested in antiquity and influenced by Leonardo da Vinci. Raphael's Saint George and the Dragon *is influenced by work Leonardo had done with horses.*

from the Roman Empire still stood there. Everything from the buildings to the city itself seemed large and impressive. The sculptures of ancient Rome were a great inspiration for Raphael. Here, he had found a place to further develop his artistic skills.

Pope Julius II

When Raphael arrived in Rome, Pope Julius was decorating his living space at the **Vatican**. Over the next few years, the pope asked Raphael to **fresco** three rooms there. It was a great honor for Raphael to work in the Vatican.

The first room Raphael worked on was called the Stanza della Segnatura. Raphael began his first set of frescoes by 1509. This set includes one of his most famous works, the *School of Athens*.

Raphael's work pleased Pope Julius. So, the pope sent away many of the other artists working at his residence. He wanted their work destroyed so that Raphael could complete everything instead. But Raphael saved some work, including a ceiling by his former master, Perugino.

Raphael painted himself second from the right in this scene from the **School of Athens**. *Perugino is to the right of him.*

The School of Athens *is often considered Raphael's best and most important work. Each individual figure leads the viewer's eye toward the center of the fresco, where Plato and Aristotle stand.*

Raphael became one of the pope's favorite artists. So, Pope Julius offered him even more work. On October 4, 1509, Raphael received a special position from the pope. His job title was *scriptor brevium*, which is a Latin term similar to "secretary." Raphael now had a permanent job and a salary.

Agostino Chigi

Banker Agostino Chigi was one of Raphael's primary customers. He was a great art **patron** of the Renaissance. Raphael worked as an **architect** on many of Chigi's buildings. And, the artist decorated many of the rooms at Villa Farnesina, Chigi's home in Rome. Raphael also created artwork for two Chigi chapels.

Just as Pope Julius had done, Chigi eventually had Raphael replace many of the artists he had previously hired. Raphael was asked to paint a room that the artist Sebastiano del Piombo had started. Piombo had worked with Michelangelo, and he became one of Raphael's rivals.

Raphael sketched this figure for a work in the Chigi chapel in Santa Maria della Pace.

Raphael created *The Triumph of Galatea* for the room. This **fresco** shows characters from Roman myths. Dated 1512, it was the first of many projects that Chigi **commissioned** from Raphael. The fresco is still found at the Villa Farnesina today.

Raphael designed statues and other artwork for the Chigi chapel in Santa Maria del Popolo.

The Architect

Pope Julius **commissioned** Raphael to create a special piece for a church in Piacenza, Italy. So from 1512 to 1513, Raphael painted the *Sistine Madonna* for the Church of San Sisto. This became one of his most popular works. In it, Pope Julius appears as the figure of Saint Sixtus.

Pope Julius died on February 21, 1513. His **successor**, Pope Leo X, was a member of the powerful Medici family. He continued the reconstruction of Rome and asked Raphael to keep working for the Catholic Church. So, Raphael was given more work to complete.

Meanwhile, Bramante had been working as chief **architect** of St. Peter's Basilica. When he died in 1514, Pope Leo asked Raphael to be the new architect at St. Peter's. It was a great challenge, but Raphael was ready for it.

The Sistine Madonna

The Sistine Madonna *shows Raphael's talent for creating beautiful faces and expressions. The gaze of each figure draws the viewer's eye around the painting. And, the figures are placed in a triangular arrangement. This emphasizes the importance of the Madonna and child at the top of the work.*

Raphael used a style called trompe l'oeil, *which is French for "deceive the eye." This is why the curtains and shelf surrounding the painting appear real. This connects the world of the painting to the world of the viewer. The figure of Saint Sixtus* (left) *appears to be pointing directly out of the canvas. This also draws the viewer into the painting.*

The Workshop

In 1517, Pope Leo asked Raphael to be in charge of preserving Roman **antiquities**. By this time, Raphael already oversaw nearly all of the church's artistic endeavors. Raphael also had **architectural** projects and **patrons** outside of the **Vatican**.

Raphael designed and worked on many of the projects assigned to him. But, Pope Leo and other patrons **commissioned** so much work that Raphael could not keep up. Luckily, Raphael had a workshop and was able to hire assistants.

Raphael's workshop was filled with many talented artists. With some projects, the assistants only helped a little. But on other assignments, they did most of the work. Still, every work kept Raphael's style. Because of his assistants, Raphael could balance his work for the pope and other patrons.

Raphael's portrait of Pope Leo and two cardinals represents three men of the powerful Medici family. The view below of the bell and the open book shows Raphael's attention to detail.

Tapestries

Pope Leo asked Raphael to design a series of ten **tapestries** for the walls of the Sistine Chapel. The tapestries would show the lives of Catholic saints, including Peter and Paul. For each work, Raphael designed a cartoon. Then, weavers in Brussels, Belgium, created the tapestries from the designs.

The finished tapestries were ready to be displayed by 1519. On important days, they were used to cover the paintings on the Sistine Chapel walls. They also helped display Pope Leo's wealth.

Despite a natural rivalry between the many Renaissance artists, Raphael respected and learned from their work. So, it had been an honor for Raphael to be **commissioned** to do work for the Sistine Chapel. His work would be mingled with the work of many other great artists. These included both his rival Michelangelo and his former master, Perugino.

Artist's Corner

Raphael

Cartoons are drawings or paintings that are created as preparation for a work of art. Usually, the cartoons are in a different medium than the final product.

Raphael's ten Sistine Chapel tapestries started out as cartoons. After the cartoons were complete, they were sent away to a weaving workshop. There, the cartoons were cut into long, wide strips. Each strip was sent to a tapestry weaver who re-created that portion of the work. Then, all the strips of tapestry were joined together. Later, the cartoons were also reassembled.

Raphael's assistants helped create most of the cartoons. However, the cartoon for *The Miraculous Draught of Fishes (below)* is thought to be Raphael's own work. Usually, cartoons were not as detailed as normal paintings, and tapestry weavers were allowed to add final details. But, Raphael did not let the cartoons leave his workshop entirely unfinished. So today, they are considered works of art on their own.

Artistic Rivalry

Near the end of his life, Raphael had a **commission** from Cardinal Giulio de Medici. Raphael was to create a painting that would be sent to a cathedral in Narbonne, France. But, Medici did not want just one painting for this cathedral. So, he hired Piombo to create a piece as well.

Pope Leo was Medici's cousin. The pope supported the idea of artistic competition. Piombo's painting, the *Raising of Lazarus*, was in competition with Raphael's the *Transfiguration*. Piombo had strong support from his mentor, Michelangelo.

Because of their enormous size, these paintings took a long time to complete. Raphael was almost finished with his when he fell ill with a fever. He died on his birthday, April 6, 1520, before the *Transfiguration* was completed.

Opposite page: *The* Transfiguration *shows Raphael's talented use of complicated lighting. The work's triangular shape draws the viewer's eyes upward. But the light on the scene below draws attention down, too.*

A Memorial

The *Transfiguration* was found in Raphael's workshop after his death. Raphael's assistant Giulio Romano later completed the painting. It was an immediate success. People agreed that both Piombo's and Raphael's paintings were amazing. However, many people preferred Raphael's.

A funeral Mass for Raphael was held at the **Vatican**. The *Transfiguration* was placed on his **bier**. Raphael was buried at the Pantheon in Rome, which was a privilege given to only the best of Rome's citizens. It was a way to honor Raphael as a part of the city he loved.

Raphael's death was near the end of the Renaissance. Leonardo had died in 1519. Chigi died less than a week after Raphael, and Pope Leo died in 1521. Raphael's art created a new standard that people were judged by for years. Many people would copy his style, but few could copy his spirit.

When Raphael arrived in Rome, he was especially impressed by the Pantheon. The ancient structure's dome was the largest built before modern times.

Glossary

altarpiece - a decorative work of art placed behind or above an altar.

antiquity - early historical times, especially before the AD 500s. Antiquities are the objects, such as art and architecture, from those times.

architect - a person who plans and designs buildings. His or her work is called architecture.

artifact - a useful object made by human skill a long time ago.

bier - a stand that holds a coffin before burial.

characteristic - a quality or a feature of something.

commission - a request to complete a work, such as a painting, for a certain person. To be commissioned is to be given such a request.

court - of or having to do with the residence, advisers, or assemblies of a ruler.

culture - the customs, arts, and tools of a nation or people at a certain time.

fresco - the art of painting on a wet surface that becomes hard when dry, such as a plaster wall.

patron - one who supports an individual or a cause with money, resources, or influence.

successor - a person who takes the place of another. Often, someone is a successor to a throne, title, estate, or office.

tapestry - a heavy woven fabric decorated with detailed designs or pictures.

Vatican - the headquarters of the Catholic Church in Rome. It is also the name of the church's government.

Saying It

Agostino Chigi - ahg-oh-STEE-noh KEE-jee
bier - BIHR
Perugia - pay-ROO-jah
Piacenza - pyah-CHEHN-sah
Pietro Perugino - PYEH-troh pehr-oo-JEE-noh
Sebastiano del Piombo - say-bahs-TYAHN-oh dayl PYAWM-boh
Urbino - ur-BEE-noh

Web Sites

To learn more about Raphael, visit ABDO Publishing Company on the World Wide Web at **www.abdopublishing.com**. Web sites about Raphael are featured on our Book Links page. These links are routinely monitored and updated to provide the most current information available.

Index